SOUL TO SONG

By

Benjamin Kwakye

Publisher's information, address:
Cissus World Press
P.O. Box 240865
Milwaukee, WI 53224
www.cissusworldpressbooks.com

ISBN: 978-0-9978689-2-0

Library of Congress Control Number: 2017942215

First Edition

Distributor:
African Books Collective Ltd
Website: http://www.africanbookscollective.com

For Samuel

Remembering a light that still shines brightly

Table of Contents

Hands of Gold

We Farmed Nightmares   7
Subtraction Toward Death   8
Time is a Murderer   9
Return of the Locusts   10
Altered Song   11
Seashore   12
Who Needs a Timepiece?   13
When the Morning Sun Arrives   14
Accra (I)   15
Accra (II)   17
Accra (III)   18
Hands of Gold   19
Gather the Griots   20
The Inhabitant   21
Foie Gras   23
Echoes of the Castles   24
A Woman of the Street   28
Defeat in the Forests   30
The Abused Road   32

Soul to Song

Soul to Song   35
A Song for Esi   36
To a Blessed Queen   38
Ode to Grace   40
The Son's Daughter   42
Song for My Beloved   44
Song of Twilight   46
Love?   48
Prosopagnosia   49

Decisive Indecisions

Enchanted Youth	51
Beware	52
Silent One	53
Final Song	55
Suspended Interview	56
History Haunting	59
The Prodigal	60
Commerce	62
Lizard from Paradise	63
Judges	67
Linguist of Angels	68
Bow Before History	69
Whispers in the Air	70
Equipoise of the Catacombs	72
Masqueraders	73
Decisive Indecisions	74

Hands of Gold

We Farmed Nightmares

Blood flowed
for farming of nightmares.

Bloodshed ambushed conscience
boomeranging queries
that darkness unveils.

If history speaks let it speak
with lessons for
hangman and guillotined alike,

else its snaking effluents seep
soiled in trail of forgotten lessons
and bloodbath of neglect.

Today transgressed youths
hold reins of governance
under self-meted sentence.

When we look to the heavens,
they echo groans of blood
in the heart of the wind.

If we let promise of honey
blind us, our children shall
forage for crumbs from
failed bequeathing
of banqueted tables.

Who carries the burden
as truth whispers of noonday anger?

Subtraction Toward Death

At birth, rain-bedded earth
yields wiggling caterpillar.

Sun-spectacled air spurs
chrysalis to anticipate.

Moon-blanketed cloud
lulls butterfly with rest—

Is this pictorial medley?

Or aorta pulsating anticipation
On rugged pathway to rigor mortis?

Time is a Murderer

East to west to
north to south
human fire scalds hope.

Hope is desert's enchantress
of mirage-oases; sadists
bringing emptied calabashes of promises.

And when the caterpillar stunts,
the chrysalis withers
and the butterfly dies before death.

Return of the Locusts

How long will locusts
gormandize your harvest?

We know seasons
changed before time.
Though Asantewaa
pounded men's chests,
their kegs were too large.

Your blossoming
stunted like yams
harvested before the sprouting.

But you have allowed
history to mock you.

The locusts came yesterday.
Sowed misbegotten seeds.

They have returned
for the harvesting.
History returns in masquerade.

Why blame the stinging bee
when your house opens its
honey-jar with door ajar?

The locusts see
the unguarded harvest
and engorged with nectar-lust
they come.

And they come.

Altered Song

They rule the world
whose song the world sings.

We traded our song for false air
to fill balloons
for transient inflation
in bogus glamour.

Sojourners from afield
took our song and altered it.

The day we sang
sieved songs
of our mothers is
the day we birthed
spiritual rottenness.

Unanchored ghosts seek habitus.

We hungered and
sang their songs for
passing air

better than melodious
legacies of our forebears.

And the voice
that teaches
the song

rules the world.

Seashore

Horizons tell time
in bronzed dawn of sunlight.

This is where angels sketch love

And gregarious ghosts silhouette
glimmers of shadows.

Here, clock is fallacy
misguiding time
in sophistry of timeliness.

Did not the sun sing noon,
the waves break space
and the hand of shadows tell time?

Air is my infinite secondhand
in the horizontal chronometer.

Who Needs a Timepiece?

Here the sunflowers lift hearts
While lights from the heavens assume
The radiance of earthly paradise.

Here morning breeze courts roses
that shiver in olfactory worship, and
ruffling silk trees explode in dance.

This is the dawn of my Africa morning.

When the Morning Sun Arrives

The hawk knows its target, but
the chick knows the ground better.

The scavenging hawk flies, but
the coop cannot be too far.

When the morning sun arrives...

Only the fool walks the desert
when the stream flows nearby.

And tomorrow ambles in quickly
Like the town crier beating a gong.

Accra (I)

When sleep morphs to waking tonic
startling feathers in my ears,
you are my waking song

in prayers of crepuscular prayer groups
in the muezzins' summons to prayer
in neighbors' cockcrows

beckoning to morning's answer
where bleating sheep
finds barking dog.

Accra,
when sleep morphs to waking tonic
startling feathers in spread-eagled ears,
you are my waking song

over splash of bathing waters
over sinewy and flabby physiques
over corrugated bath floors

ghosting neglect
conjoining stench of excreta
and open sewers.

Accra,
when sleep morphs to waking tonic
startling feathers in spread-eagled ears,
you are my waking song,

and before you I prostrate
at the Korle Lagoon,
to breathe life and ask:
how shall I describe thee?

Stench of primordial depth,
Or echo of celestial nightingales
Regaling sun and heat?

Accra (II)

This is the serenade of the progeny,
where survival is a gift &
vehicular conversations chorus
the sinking sun.

Accra,
my wedding song
my ballad at twilight

What haven't I loved about you?
Amassing bats on trees
thawing heat & the horizon's
darkness bearing light

These are your songs of love
promulgating predictions.
Who else but you
could accommodate
makeshift tents for release
of satyric appetites
where the dank air offers the sea
its salt for taste?

Accra,
dirge solemner than the atenteben's
dirge deeper than hate, yet
stronger than love...
Your nights claw over waters and land.

Accra,
dirge committed to morning's rebirth,
while night wows us all with an ancient voice.

Accra (III)

City of false exhaustion.
Lover of night's emanations:
    --moonbeam's lunatic focus
    --bats' nocturne with sleepy sparrows
    --traditions of power failures.

Years on I still remember
the fiery familial gatherings
joining the nocturnal sketches
of your elegies:
    --lovers' coital climaxes,
    --youths' twirls on club floors,
    --all night prayers of the spiritually inclined.

Day and night my lifts
from the graveyard of nostalgia
this tireless city
romancing its subjects
with the mystery of its
inexhaustible in-exhaustion.

Hands of Gold

Your faults bemoaned, I too will weep;
Yet, today, I recite sweet verses,
Shining stars in bleak nights of despair,
Even if belying your crimson sweat,
The bloody petals that are your pain.

A belly laden with wealth,
a garner of hope.

Could your verses be said in uranium
And your tunes chanted in platinum?

Could your songs be sung in diamonds
And your melodies hummed in petroleum?

Could your stanzas be composed in chrome
And your lines read in bauxite?

The rhapsody of monsoon winds
Trumpet sweet dreams, presages of progress
In tomorrow's dawning winds.

Write me your verses in hands of gold
Even if the future surfaces discordant—
A medley of thorns, still it beckons
As hope's silhouette nods its head yes.

Gather the Griots

Gather the griots,
Write me your verses in hands of gold.
Even if the future surfaces discordant—
A medley of thorns, still it beckons
As hope's silhouette nods its head yes.

Gather the griots,
Under the bellowing baobab, neem and oak.
Let them write verses in hands of gold.
Ancestors' songs, beckoning of nomadic progeny,
Riding astride clouds.

Gather the griots,
Gather the children too and let sages
Write me sweet verses in gold's hands.
Their gray hairs are tributes to wisdom.
Their stories of old are interspersed with proverbs—
Sweet proverbs presaging progress
In tomorrow's dawning winds.

The Inhabitant

He cowers from the blare of tooting horn,
trembles at buildings scratching space,
flees from crowded marketplaces,
staggers over paved streets
and curses sunlight distilled
through decorative sunflower and bougainvillea.

He catches fever from perfumed skins
and coughs from stove-made dishes.

In insomniac stare he shrieks
at the jaundiced sun and moon
of city luminosities.

Home is where the mahogany and oak
converge as shelter,
the shrub is carpet,
and the river a pathway.

Disheveled hair is crown
and aromatic petrichor of
rainfall-sketched mud is cologne.

Sun and moon are soothing caresses of
velvet-gloved masseuses.

He wears lightning and bears thunder
with feline insouciance.

He knows the lion's ways
and teaches the parrot songs.

He holds up the sky

with a judoka's energy.

He has studied the breathing of stars
And the moods of the forests.

Be humble before this child.
He will lead you in new pathways.

Foie Gras

My ears engorge on
saccharine-sounds
of their percussionist.

My eyes are serenaded
with ocular meat
of their desires.

My throat is gorged
with ingestions
of their philosophies.

Their flatulence is my oxygen.

I am the fattened calf
with weakened habitus
engorged for the sacrifice
of their commerce
and ready for their slaughter.

Echoes of the Castles

From Coast of Gold
the castle still speaks
past erosions of history

echoes of guttural
protests of pain

talons scrawling
protest eaten by cramping walls
where they shackled them as beasts
for the slaughter of spirit

Blinded as darkness
in dungeons of no return

shadows
simulations of death

to sleep sitting
to sleep head-bowed
between strangers' legs

spirit-stripped and lashed

to yielding wombs

rape an escape
this or death

for even death wept
at the sight
it could not behold
and took souls
with trembling hands

with face turned away

With those living becoming ghosts
in the bestial wallow of

vomit
blood
sweat
tears
feces

Soup for the devil
Above them rose Sunday's prayers

But the ghosts were in gestation
to beget living lions who roared
through bestial burdens

Acts offensive to nature
But the lions lived

Years have sojourned
and returned

aged

And still the walls utter
guttural moans

There is no sangfroid here
Every spirit that visits weeps

It calls forth
Cape Coast calls forth

Elmina calls forth

I am your castle

From walls of stone
the voice of death
outlasts the facades
of ageless walls

The dead stand to remind you
You who became ghosts across
aqueous graveyards of the Atlantic

Now in your leonine season
you can live again

You borne of living ghosts
whose spirits live
in the crucible of wounded blood
I call you

You whose lawns bore
the fiery cross

whose eyes witnessed
hoods sporting the hangman's rope
I call you

The spirit of the survivors speaking
from my walls call you

Dip desiccated tongues in the troughs
that have widened to full ocean
instead of bread of sorrows
make bread from sorrow

Stand Stand Stand

Ghana calls you
Cape Coast calls you
Elmina calls you

The door of no return
is the door of return

Amistad is liaison
of punctuated times
not their chasm

The oceanic tombstones
carry the pilgrims back
bearing them over sea and cloud

The children swim
gyrating welcome motions

Groaning shadows have begat lions

Screams from the walls give
roaring voice to lions

And living ghosts have begat lions
roaring and roaring with the voice
of the Atlantic

A Woman of the Street

If I didn't tell you about her,
You wouldn't know.
Her head bowed low,
She looked into the ground
As though it held deep wonder.

Draw close, you will see:
Her hair sprawled dry and kinky,
Her face bone-sculptured,
And her lips cracked.

Her nostrils dilated,
As if breathing dire hunger.

The body of shriveled flesh
Yielded under tattered clothes
Dyed deep by begrimed streets
She roamed.

Her feet fell into eroded sandals
And she walked with death's stagger.

I averted my gaze, pushing my way past.

But wait! I caught her gaze
From sudden turn of assured head,
Heard cymbals of divine orchestra
Piercing into me, reflecting me,
Holding mirrors of me.

My heart became oarsmen
And I looked deeper.

Her eyes held a million phrases.

She smiled with sacerdotal grace.

How could she, one so placed
Find strength for such elegant speech?

Defeat in the Forests

Humming forests glided me
through tunes of grasshoppers,
stentorian guffaw of lions,
genuflecting praying mantis,
hoards of bees building honey,
and a bamboo walking
with elephant grass.

The eagle, the hawk, the vulture,
the dove and the sparrow

beat vapor-hisses of snakes
into danceable rhythms.

Their voices unearthed
the earth's drumming hearts.

This, the peacock blended
into melting colors.

The palms of earth bore
cheetahs' gallop
where gazelle ran zigzaggedly

from the pursuit.

Sounds of the forests rose
in thunderous rhythms

then fell into silent din
of hardened ears.

Heaven bowed, held earth steady.

Kinship of celestial sincerity.

My bow and arrow throbbed
but beat out of rhythm
with the earth's hearts.

I steadied my quivering aim.
The silence stood cruel.

I could hear chattering drums
prognosticating sweet demise
of my game.

My aim perfected by sinewy arm,
the arrow lurched forward,
whistled past praying grasshoppers
and walking bamboo.

The hush of the forests ossified.

My arrow flew aimless,
as if in sightless wonder.

Then drove back.

A boomerang driving
for my heartless mind.

I fled the forests.

And the peacock sang.

The Abused Road

When you see me in black tar
And trucks negotiate my curves,
Standing in lethal dance,
With careless steering ease;

When taxi drivers corrode
My beautiful body with tireless play,

Don't call me a prostitute.

When you see my edges
Lined with repulsive soil
And fires set my tar weak
Or caked by droughty heart;

When pedestrians abuse my delicate flesh
And I groan under muddy footwear,

Don't call me filthy.

When you see my abused beauty
Tangled in phlegm from choked nostrils
Or spittle from unwashed mouths
And the trash of many months
Line my landscape with their stench,

Don't shun me.

I nourished you with my child's sweat.
I bore you with the wealth from my soils
Even when you impoverished my back.

But today I am the despised hero
Who forgot to claim her due.

But when you see my body
Avalanched by unsightly holes
And my pools are filled
With rain from an unsympathetic sky,

They are not the tears of my dirge
But the rebirth of my weary body
And of my mourned soul.

Soul to Song

Soul to Song

Body pressed against body—
Interlocked like webs,
Moan marries meshed moan,
Becoming the soundtrack
Of the almost hushed hours
When only grasshoppers dare speak,
As messengers of deities,
Their night-spirited choruses.

Like spirits exchange spirits
In the midnight hours,
The glib presages
Of the ecstatic gifts of dawn
Soon to come
And break our love-panting
With its fowl-crows.

And then
Watery mists of morning
Wet their grass mats with dew—
The spit of gods that collect
On our naked bodies
Whose night-kneaded crevices
Are the spittoon of those deities
Showering their blessings.

The gods salivated
The night we made them voyeurs,
Showed them our love-dance,
The feasting on bodies
That permitted the feasting of spirits
That made them drool wide-mouthed
In the sacred depths of their dessicated forests.

A Song for Esi

There is the movement
that beats its unseen drums
as if nature meshed
all rhythms into one body;

the face smiling deeper
than crevices of mountains,
rescuing me from Age's
graveyards of despair
into the secure palms
of matrimonial birth.

They may try to appraise
your worth with words
but how crass, this exercise,
when you can only
be measured by infinite
emanations of hearts,
excesses of spirits
and boundlessness of souls.

If the leaves were
to flutter in the night
and the moon glow
dim its libidinal shade,
you would be the air
that catches the sun
past legs of the neem
and feet of the mahogany
through impermeable
thatches and sieves
to the unsung chests
of sleeping masses.

Divine handiwork
expressed in perfection,
the voice at noon
that seduces the sun
so it lingers,
comfortable as skin
on our bodies;
the hand that holds
the night's missed dreams
to free them into the stars
of the waking dawn.

Beyond the gift
that was promised Adam

Perfected in the unsullied
refinery of time,
your presence is my blood;
your love, my air.

To a Blessed Queen

Applause of angels, genuflection of mortals
To Shira, blessed queen,
We bid you Welcome.

Neither sound nor gesture made or invented,
Not voice or trumpet or cymbal, suffices
To unveil this perfection of the perfect.

The lexicographer whimpers, stymied for words
At the topography of joy, fully contoured,
That only heart and spirit can discern.

Announced on signal of a device's assertion,
Then the magic of ultrasound speaking—
Ascertained as a dot on paper
As Pa and Ma joined to thank Him,
With one accord to acknowledge
That love had wrought a beginning
Of perfection, wonderfully and fearfully made.

Oh, what labor of love as prologue:
Regurgitation and morning discomforts—
Ma, the most valiant of soldiers.

Then pediatricians and nurses and
Lactation agents, and tubes, needles and monitors...

But you winked at familiar voices of Ma and Pa
As if to say, *What are they worried about?*
Yes, we heard you in the beginning as you announced:

*All great things are costly
And we bargain with adversity for greatness.*

And our hearts churned with love.

And now you survey as a monarch
Your face an amalgam of us.

If beauty had a name, would they have to look far?

Nana, Shira, Esi, Akosua, Kwamette...
Blessed among the blessed.
Let orchestral tunes play in celestial places;
Let love sing to the awaiting world.

You will embrace it
With pride but not arrogance,
Boldness but not foolishness.

Nana, you will rise as the queen you are.
Set Him above all and walk in His light.

Never take shelter in the obscure corners.
He has given you the bright candle
Now go boldly and light the world.

Shira, to bless and be blessed
To love and be loved...

Shira, blessed queen,

We bid you

Welcome.

Ode to Grace

You whispered in the spirit and we answered,
Your spirit adorning ours before birth.
Assuredly you said Faith and we said Jeede.

But the glittering gold needed further furbishing
And assuredly you added Grace
And we said Adoma.

Spirit that shines as with galactic presence;
Regal and on time you peered into the space
Of your kingdom, hurrying to survey your conquest.

And the conquered rejoiced
When the first cry spelled victory.

We held you aloft—can such immeasurable joy
Be repeated after the first child?

You answered yes, bestowing it in liberal quantities.
We imbibed it with spiritual gourds, nodding—

What privilege! What privilege! What privilege!

We could hear: Here I am! Here I am! Here I am!

And night was your day. And so it was. And so it is,
For your light is brighter than the noonday.

You shall call from things that never were
And you will not ask why;
You will ask why not.

Impossible is a banished mirage.

Daughter of ever increasing beauty,
Carried on the sinews of faith.
You are who you are: the heart's illuminant.
And singing independence, you reach,
Arms ajar, to embrace Sister and Mother and Father.

And we embrace you, daughter of faith!
We embrace you, sister of grace!

The Son's Daughter

Night's argument for luster
began losing its water
when she stole light
from the encircling darkness

to ease the strain of
travel and travail cross-country.

When Chicago closed its arms
for a California welcoming
you were the sun
the darkness miscomprehended

Calling before you were summoned
because you knew the smell of the times.

A time for everything,
everything for the time,

Kris. Kristo. Kristodia.

For the Son, you called your name.

And your confirmation before midnight
unfurled morning like truths of stardust.

You set your pace, Pacesetter.

Ahead of your time,
Daughter of the Son.

You are the fragrance of noon
altering aroma of the petrichor
where flowers blossom

from sweet pollination of your smile.

Who can withhold love
From the whisper of your voice?

Daughter of love.
Daughter of Margaret.
Daughter of Benjamin.

Pearl-begotten
From the right hand...

You saw the beauty
of the mysterious trinity
and you carried it
by the number of your birth.

Song for My Beloved

Elders have gathered
in the courtyard.

With frowning voices
they call my beloved out
for judgment.

She comes
but unbowed head

She has tested time and love,
she has tasted time and love
and she has loved me.

They want the admission of guilt:
Regal blood does
not mix with proletarian blood,
except in the tabooing
influences of coarse cravings,
except under lustful
injection of forbidden love.

But she has not wavered.

She is her own defense.
Her aubade is soothing vapor.
But she will not smother you.

Her afternoon tongue
is as candlelight.
It inflames but does not conflagrate
to demonstrate its power.

It knows the wages
of famous applause
implodes in the ashes of its transience.

Her love:
It heals but does not engulf.
It does not need validation,
only complementation.

In her nighttime tongue
her streams will ease you
but she will not drown you.

My beloved draws closer
to the guillotine of their tongues.

Her smile is antidote
to fear of lustful consumption.
It is what seizes the courtyard
and steals the light from skies.

Such love cannot die,
for if it should die,
hope will find its cemetery,
morning will go to the graveyards
afternoon to the tombstones
and evening to the catacombs,

and the blood of her love
will wake in the morning,
judging the judges for murdering life.

Song of Twilight

In the prologue
leafs recline

in the evening
dressed in the gold

where the weathered
rays of sun
meet the horizon.

Is this what it means
to die and resurrect
in the glow of something
transcendent?

In the interregnum
I am dead, I know;
but I am alive because
in the surrender
I know I no longer live.

The epilogue
is in the imminent opening
where fireflies glitter
and lunar rays fall
and stars pierce
the heavenly darkness.

Darkness is spurious
for in me there
is a new light.

And surely in its darkness

it shines brighter
than afternoon luster.

Love?

Lying under the bright shadows
of tall pirouetting trees
vibrating to the rhythm of the wind,
encompassed, were contagious spirits.

They were clutched in bright embrace
like magnetized souls, love-clad,
its sea engulfing the amorous whales,

I could see their world lost to the world,
two infants in ethereal innocence,
the milky way, their path,
I could feel the vibration of love.

Yet when the lassitude of the shore,
the chilly current of the rest,
caught the strides in my steps
into frozen icicles

hovering around them everywhere,
anon, were big strands of discord
taming the love I had felt,
entrapped in the manacles of the mundane.

Prosopagnosia

I love the empty faces,
the indistinguishable.

One for the other, all for one.
Pity my simplicity
where I can't discern
valleys and shadows of faces
or the seasons of their emotions—
the frown of hate
or facial bouquets of
aquamarine sparkle.

But this facelessness...

After history blends time
in the ovens of experience,

Wonder if this is the key
To love agape.

Decisive Indecisions

Enchanted Youth

He coughed blood
thicker than molasses,
this youth gormandized
on flesh of the dead.

His story is not
the trail of forgotten lessons,
nor bloodbath of neglect.

This transgressed youth
holding the reins of governance
under our own sentence.

Even as his blood litigates us
from pains of time.

Beware

History goes and comes
like a bloodied boomerang.

Unless we consciously bend
its blood-soaked currents
in the courts of conscience,

hope is a calabash of
promises chaperoning life.

Silent One

This old man...

Masqueraded by air
of time to become air:

Time provokes him
to be wind.

You don't hear him.
You experience him.

He molds time
with history's curricula.

He has seen great wars
and he has sung peace.

Neither raindrop
nor sunlight
can mine his secrets.

He sang nations for hope
and spewed them out
in despair.

And still he hopes
for Armah's beautyful ones.

Like blood.
Often unseen.
Seldom heard,

But disturbed,

gushes red anger
to extinguish life.

There is too much power
in his silences.
This old man.

Beware. What you do
not know
will kill you.

Final Song

The eagle lost its head
because the snail
ate its song.

I am the song
that snarls at the evening sun

the song
that eats the air.

I am the song
that kills eagles

though I may lie dormant
under the mangrove

hibernate like a python

I conduct the ferocious storm
at the noonday party.

The plague
that will not be placated.

I am the song
that killed the eagle.

Sing me and die.

Suspended Interview

This, the currency of despair:
Rejection letters piled on cluttered desk;
Rejections boomeranged to
Become necrophilic companion
Of fast-paced dying hope.

Was my heart forever the cuspidor
In which employers spat rejections?

Then came the unexpected call—
A jarring summons in surrender of quiet evening.
The perfunctory introduction followed, then:

You have an impressive resume
And I have the perfect job for you.

The announcement closed the distance—
This, the voice of an angel.
In this moment of miraculous kinship,
The world suspended its axial spin—
A miracle unfolding its mystery.
Here was the end of restless months
Of resumes dispensed in rubbish heap
Of mysterious cyberspace,
And mountain dustbins
Of moribund snail footed post.
But now this beckoning promise—

Sir, when should I come to your office
For the interview? I asked.

That won't be necessary;
A phone interview is sufficient.
As I have said, your resume has impressed me.

56

So we spoke on, my experiences compressed
Into thirty minutes of questions and answers.

You are so impressive. By the way,
Your name. I was wondering. Is it Polish?

I paused, now on quacking ground, full of concern.
His question, what relevance to my ability?
Would my resume cease to impress in its quicksand?
No, sir, I said, it's African.

He paused, and I waited as
Silent seconds ticked into painful seconds
Into pause of misconceived pregnancy.
Then came the whispered voice:

I will call you soon.

Deep stains in the air.

And then died the dial tone.
Another hope miscarried?

I waited.
I waited.
I waited.

I will call you soon kept hope's memory alive.

But fifteen years have become its closing noose.
Still, whenever the phone rings, the noose shakes
As I wait for the ear of my absentee angel to ask:

Mandela left the walls of Robben Island,
Anan reigned over nations united,

Obama wore the face of a nation,
But you, sir, what took you so long?

History Haunting

Car stopped. Presages of death.
Hands on steering wheel.
Internal lights illuminated.
Don't shoot. Don't shoot.
But in the muzzle
Are ancient pronouncements
Masquerading still in modern prayers to Satan

      Through the laughter of angels,
      after church bells have rung,
      through the melodious aubade,
      past missa cantata,
      come the tears of angels,
      when warped apothecaries of hate
      dispense toxins of spiritual rot—
      the masked grotesqueries of love,
      this love that spills from the face only,
      without root in the core of hearts.

      Satan hears such prayers,
      soaks them in sponges
      squeezed into rainfalls
      of earthly hell.

      Better the face of the devil
      than a chameleon-smile.

Time and times coalesce.

The trigger is just
History unreformed.

The Prodigal

The sojourner—
By the candlelight he crouches,
hunger dimmed face moaning alienation.
He forages for the breadcrumbs
of corpulent indigenes.

He has come in silhouette only
for his bones and flesh trigger disquiet
and many perspire when he raises his head
and they see the purpose of his eyes,
preferring him to stay in the margins
content to receive morsels
of selective noblesse oblige.

His head has worn crowns before.
But abandoned crowns cast a shadow.

He crouches, his way lost in the way.

His roofless house gorges on rainfall's mercy.

Roof your house.
Pampered passersby command.

They mistake him for a drunkard
like stanzas mangled in alcoholic stupor.
They think his scent stinks,
Synonymizing difference and stench.

If he is now denied, how can the progeny
join the festive table?

The prince has fled his kingdom
and even the pigsty

rejects his lamentations for rest.

Do not tarry then, for a crown still awaits
the prodigal prince in his abandoned kingdom

Where, even if he cannot run, he can walk;
if he cannot sing, he can talk.
And none winces when he passes by
or holds court to fathom him.

And he hears ballads in the dark.

Time has long passed
and the way back
is fogged with darkness.

But experience of rejection is light
in the womb of encircling clouds.

Rainfall is a zygote
of the heavens for earth.

Rain falls latterly
for latterly seeding,

drinking tarried germination,
when the deprived pluck
the riches of the ending harvest.

Commerce

Scavengers prowl
where streets churn ghosts—
mining factories of deaths
piquing the pilgrim's interest
for a yellowed tale for pages
consumed in the ignoramus'
appetite for exotic yarns.

What interest if we all breathe air?
What salability if we all drink water?
What esteem bestowed if we all eat food?

How boring to look
into the everyday-album!

Sameness is somnolence.

No, the mendacious
must manufacture a tale
or find one and salinize it
for the vampire who lives
on the blood of otherness.

Lizard from Paradise

How many deaths shall a man die
before he finally dies?
Today, I died a little—

the death
that snuffs without killing.

If I were a lizard from paradise
he may have shaken my hand,

But I was merely coifed
in a suit well pressed for the meeting.

We had met at least
three times
three times
three times
in previous meetings

He, the group leader
who'd mentioned me by name
for masturbatory discourse.

This morning,
we,
among five, waited
waited in the lobby for the elevator,

His suit worth a thousand more
than mine.

I smiled, adjusted my tie
and extended my hand for the taking.

But he stared
then turned his back to me
and walked away.

If I were a lizard from paradise
he may have shaken my hand

But I was merely coifed in a suit
well pressed for the meeting.

The five glances at me were
as five thousand arrows of opprobrium
for deserving the snub
of my solicitation for a handshake.

The concierge considered my face,
puzzled, squeezed a smile
aiming to shrink my humiliation
in the crucible of shared humanity.

I raced into the elevator—
the first time must have been a mistake.

I extended my hand again,
straightened my tie
and mentioned his name.

With squinted eyes he declared
 "Look, you've got the wrong guy."

My hand in the air.
My hand in the air.
My hand in the air.

His hands by his sides.
His head ready to spin away.

If I were a lizard from paradise
he may have shaken my hand,

But I was merely coifed
in a suit well pressed for the meeting.

My smile long dead,
I mentioned my name.
"I am on your team, sir."

He looked at me again.
"Oh," he said, "Sorry. I meant nothing by that."

And now unsheathed:
the hand so delicately preserved
persevered from my handshake.

The grip was firm
Prolonged

But it did not inspire paradise.

The seismic quake in my belly,
the volcano, the avalanche

Churned.

Today, the man died a little.
Today, he died a little.

How many deaths must a man suffer
before he finally dies?

If I were a lizard from paradise
he may have shaken my hand,

Shaken my hand
in the very first instance
of possible embrace.

But I was merely coifed in a suit
well pressed for his meeting.

Judges

They
cannot see
that air needs winds for breath

That empathy is the oil
that greases the creaking
wheels of justice.

For both
judge and judged...

Linguist of Angels

Death is the linguist of angels.

Still, if I grieve,
grief is wind.

I wept.

And Jesus wept.

Therefore, I will grieve,
and in the quiet night hear

your voice in
hiccups of silence.

Beyond sorrowful mists,
I will see your spirit
negotiating with the linguist
for passage past the linguist.

And Jesus wept.

So too I will weep,
but in weeping,
knowing love does not
self-assassinate,
look to Lazarus

And down by the stream
lay my head to rest

and study grief no more.

Bow Before History

A bow before those
Transparent canvasses
At times translucent

Modern tributaries of ancient wars
Fought and lost and won and...

Mind and body and spirit
And rhyme and dreams

Have replayed on
Unending landscapes

And so with such
Tinkering and worship

Perhaps something historic
Something profound unveils
As time gyres around me
From dimmed depths of history
Flowing from extending abysses
Of memories' dwelling places

To reward worshippers
Of times past

But time is a sham.
Time is the paradox
Of here and of nothingness.

And if hunters hunt carcasses
What will the living feast on?

Whispers in the Air

Grandpa told me to tell my tales.

Every generation has a song.
Every generation has a dream.

Every song sings a dream.

A tale untold is a dream
in search of an interpretation.

A song unsung is blood
seeking veins for clothing.

A history muffled is unbound spirit
seeking a body to inhabit.

Troubadours are hijackers laying ambush
to sing my dream, my song, my history.

But no one interprets my time better than me,
for time is a liar because history is its linguist.
And both time and history are vacuums
And people inhabit their voices.

I am the linguist of my song, my time, my dream.

Therefore, I write into
the wind for whispers of angels.

A song is never lost
even without human chorusing.

The echoes of the hills
feed the soul to sing.

And somewhere, some people will hear
that still voice carried in the windless air

And my song will become theirs
because it'd be their song

Until then meaningless as passing wind
because of the contortion of alien tones.

Equipoise of the Catacombs

Even here there are incisors
and molars and canine variations.

Granpapa's tomb
bears no flowery carpeting
or ornate bouquets.

Just the song of his life.

We have wept,
as they have.

Their tears are not fattened
or their grief reversed
whose loved ones rest
in luxuriant catacombs.

Perhaps we weep
a refrain for joy
for a richer life
that lived from love

While their dirge is discorded
by a life that lived
from wealth withheld
from the laboring
and misapplied to the debauched.

Wealth, where is your sting?

Masqueraders

In the quiet of morning
what if we asked...

What if the bird's chirp
is lamentation for the dead night?

What if the sun of noontide
is façade of angry fire
over morning's despair?

What if the breeze of leisured evening
is mask over strains of daytime?

What if the moonlight
Is rage tampered by clouds
Over anger of night's diabolical opus?

What if we asked?

Decisive Indecisions

I

Ink dries on open pages.

From blankness, word weds thought
to abandon despair's authority
and weave crisp images,
alchemy of mind and spirit
whose limbs swing
wide as oceanic memory.

Eyes extend to coming horizons,
thought feeds on thought
in deep spiritual mines,
devoured within gourds
that oil creation from wet ink
to living lines and pages.

Why search for muses
in love's darkened spaces
or the abysses of despair
when the oasis springs
from nectars of the wandering wonderer?

II

So I go seeking nectar.

Question! Question! My mind wonders.
Question! Question! My mind wanders.
Pinpoint inaccuracies. Aimless accuracies.

Indecision?

Aspersions on wondering,
wandering minds
sow seeds of indolent thoughts.

Intellectual thrombosis.
Malodorous mental flatulence.
Cerebral rigor mortis.

Question. Challenge. Wonder.
Wander. Question. Challenge.
There, in the heathendom of words
and in their gyrating pulse,
the sphygmograph of ambulatory thought,
hides tomorrow's deoxyribonucleic acid.

So dare me. Disturb me.
I too will be your provocateur.

Indecision, you say?
Tant mieux.

Wander to the left; wonder to the right;
Wander and wonder in the center.

I am the garbologist of mental cobwebs.

Printed in the United States
By Bookmasters